LIGHTNING BOLT BOOKS™

Dangerous Blizzards

Lola Schaefer

Lerner Publications • Minneapolis

Thank you, Jason Thistlethwaite, University of Waterloo

Lerner Publications Company
An imprint of Lerner Publishing Group, Inc.
241 First Avenue North
Minneapolis, MN 55401 USA

For reading levels and more information, look up this title at www.lernerbooks.com.

Main body text set in Billy Infant Regular. Typeface provided by SparkType.

Library of Congress Cataloging-in-Publication Data

Names: Schaefer, Lola M., 1950– author.
Title: Dangerous blizzards / Lola Schaefer.
Description: Minneapolis, MN : Lerner Publications, [2022] | Series: Lightning bolt books - earth in danger | Includes bibliographical references and index. | Audience: Ages 6–9 | Audience: Grades 2–3 | Summary: "Blizzards are severe snowstorms that include very strong winds and can extend for miles. Readers learn how to spot blizzards and how to stay safe and warm if they find one on their doorsteps"— Provided by publisher.
Identifiers: LCCN 2021025237 (print) | LCCN 2021025238 (ebook) | ISBN 9781728441436 (library binding) | ISBN 9781728447919 (paperback) | ISBN 9781728444802 (ebook)
Subjects: LCSH: Blizzards—Juvenile literature.
Classification: LCC QC926.37 .S298 2022 (print) | LCC QC926.37 (ebook) | DDC 363.34/925—dc23

LC record available at https://lccn.loc.gov/2021025237
LC ebook record available at https://lccn.loc.gov/2021025238

Manufactured in the United States of America
1-49914-49757-9/8/2021

Table of Contents

Blizzards Blow

The temperature drops. Snow falls and falls. The wind blows. The air is cold.

More snow falls. The wind makes drifts. The drifts grow tall. Snow covers roads and yards. This is a blizzard.

Heavy snowfall in West London

A blizzard is a snowstorm that lasts at least three hours. **Air and ground temperatures are under 32°F (0°C).**

°C

°F

50

40

30

20

10

0

10

20

30

120

100

80

60

40

20

0

20

20

When temperatures are very low, water freezes and it can snow.

During a blizzard, the wind blows more than 35 miles (56 km) an hour. The blowing snow makes a whiteout. A whiteout makes it difficult to see anything over 0.25 miles (0.4 km) away.

Snow in New York City

How Blizzards Begin

Warm, wet air comes from the south. Cold, dry air comes from the north. When they meet, it forms a front.

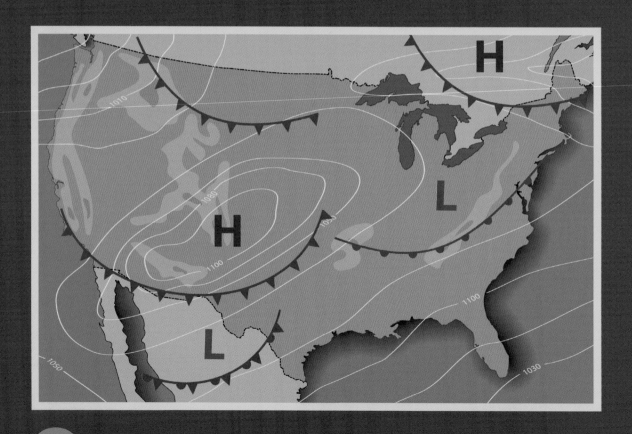

The warm, wet air rises over the cold air and clouds form. When the air is colder than freezing, precipitation falls as snow from the clouds.

A boy and his snowman

Blizzards can form in both the city and the country.

Strong winds reach 35 to 60 miles (56 to 97 km) an hour. All of the snow blows around. So much snow makes it unsafe to be outside.

Because of climate change, blizzards will become more extreme. **This means blizzards will last longer, with more snow and stronger winds.**

Kumtag Desert, Turpan, China

Dangerous Blizzards

It is dangerous for animals and people to be outside during a blizzard. Walking becomes difficult. It is easy to get lost during a whiteout.

Stay in during blizzards, and bundle up if you go out on a cold day.

If the cold air touches your bare skin or if you are outside for too long, you can get frostbite. Frostbite can damage the skin and should be checked out by a doctor.

People who are outside in a blizzard might suffer from hypothermia. This is when a person's body temperature falls below 95°F (35°C). The person may die if they don't warm up.

It's important to keep your body temperature warm enough.

Snowdrifts can cover doors and windows.

Blizzards make heavy piles of snow. People or animals can get trapped in the snow. They can get too cold and freeze.

staying safe

You can stay safe during a blizzard by staying inside. Keep pets inside. Listen to the radio or watch a news station for updates on the storm.

During the winter, keep extra food and water in your home. Make sure you have flashlights and blankets or sleeping bags in case the power goes out.

Supplies like this can help you survive.

Extra clothes can help keep you warm in an emergency.

If your family has a car, keep an emergency kit in it. Pack warm clothes, coats, blankets, bottled water, and snacks.

Blizzards are part of nature. They cannot be prevented. But we can plan ahead. Be ready to stay safe and take care of one another.

Be sure conditions are safe before playing outside.

I Survived a Blizzard

Ted Schaefer was heading home during the Indiana blizzard of 1978. He couldn't see the road because of blowing snow. He accidentally drove into a ditch. Someone stopped and helped him get out of the ditch. At home, the winds blew 40 to 60 miles (64 to 97 km) per hour for three days. It snowed more than 20 inches (51 cm). Two weeks later, the roads were open again. Because someone stopped to help him, Schaefer survived Indiana's worst recorded blizzard.

Blizzard Facts

- Just 1 inch (2.5 cm) of precipitation can produce 13 inches (33 cm) of wet snow or more than 40 inches (102 cm) of dry, powdery snow.

- In 1972, a blizzard blasted through Iran for one week. The storm dropped 10 to 26 feet (3 to 8 m) of snow.

- Thundersnow is when lightning and thunder occur during a snowstorm. They tend to happen in late winter or early spring.

- Farmers have to prepare for blizzards. Years ago they ran ropes or fences between their homes and their barns. Then they didn't get lost or stranded when feeding animals that had to stay in the barns during a blizzard.

Glossary

climate change: long-term changes in global temperature due to human and natural activity

front: the edge of a mass of cold or warm air

frostbite: damage to parts of the body, such as fingers, toes, or ears, by extreme cold

hypothermia: a significant and potentially dangerous drop in body temperature

precipitation: water falling from the sky as rain, sleet, hail, or snow

update: the latest information

whiteout: a blizzard that blows thick snow that reduces visibility to almost zero

Learn More

Britannica Kids: Blizzard
https://kids.britannica.com/kids/article
/blizzard/476228

Facts Just for Kids: Blizzards
https://www.factsjustforkids.com/weather-facts
/blizzard-facts-for-kids/

Kim, Carol. *Dangerous Floods*. Minneapolis: Lerner
Publications, 2022.

London, Martha. *Blizzards*. Minneapolis: DiscoverRoo,
2020.

Rathburn, Betsy. *Blizzards*. Minneapolis: Bellwether
Media, 2020.

Weather Wiz Kids: Winter Storms
https://www.weatherwizkids.com/weather-winter
-storms.htm

Index

Photo Acknowledgments

Image credits: V_Sot_Visual_Content/Shutterstock.com, p. 4; Jon Paul Perry/Arranginglight
.com/Getty Images, p. 5; Marian Weyo/Shutterstock.com, p. 6; Tetra Images/Getty
Images, p. 7; YULIYA SHAVYRA/Getty Images, p. 8; Jose Luis Pelaez/The Image Bank/Getty
Images, p. 9; Zabavna/Shutterstock.com, p. 10; Xuanyu Han/Moment/Getty Images, p. 11;
justoomm/Shutterstock.com, p. 12; LightField Studios/Shutterstock.com, p. 13; Yuganov
Konstantin/Shutterstock.com, p. 14; Rob Kints/Getty Images, p. 15; Konstantin Aksenov/
EyeEm/Getty Images, p. 16; photka/Shutterstock.com, p. 17; sockagphoto/Shutterstock
.com, p. 18; Jose Luis Pelaez Inc/Getty Images, p. 19.